THE HISTORY DETECTIVE INVESTIGATES

D1585749

BRITAIN AT WAR
WOMEN'S WAR

Martin Parsons

WAYLAND

Editor: Jason Hook
Designer: Simon Borrough
Cartoon artwork: Richard Hook

First published in 1999 by Wayland Publishers Ltd, 61 Western Road,
Hove, East Sussex, BN3 1JD, England

© Copyright 1999 Wayland Publishers Ltd
Find Wayland on the Internet at http://www.wayland.co.uk
This edition published in 2000 by Wayland Publishers Ltd
British Library Cataloguing in Publication Data
Parsons, Martin
    Women's war. – (The history detective investigates. Britain at war)
    1. World War 1939–1945 – Women – Great Britain – Juvenile literature
    2. World War, 1939–1945 – War work – Great Britain – Juvenile literature
    3. World War, 1939–1945 – Participation, Female – Juvenile literature
    I. Title II. Hook, Richard
    941'.084'082
ISBN 0 7502 2845 8

Printed and bound in Italy by G. Canale & C SpA, Turin
Cover pictures: (bottom) land girls in 1941; (top-centre) a WVS badge; (top-right) a government
recruitment poster.
Title page: An air-raid warden and a nurse after an air raid.

Picture Acknowledgements: The publishers would like to thank the following for permission to
reproduce their pictures: Doreen Ellis 14 (top); E.T. Archives 27 (top); Hulton Getty Images *cover*
(bottom), *title page*, 6 (top), 8, 12 (top), 13, 14 (bottom), 15, 16 (bottom), 18 (right), 20 (top), 21
(bottom), 24 (right); Imperial War Museum, London 7 (bottom-right), 11 (left); John Frost
Historical Newspapers 25 (left); Peter Newark's Pictures 4 (bottom), 19 (bottom), 21 (top);
Popperfoto 5, 6 (bottom), 7 (top, bottom-left), 10 (top), 18 (left), 19 (top), 20 (bottom), 23, 24
(left), 27 (bottom), 29 (bottom); Press and Journal 4 (top); Public Record Office *cover* (top-right),
9, 10 (bottom), 16 (top), 22 (right), 29 (top); Robert Opie 12 (bottom); Science and Society
Picture Library 22 (left), 25 (right), 26, 28; Topham 17 (bottom); Wayland Picture Library
(photography by Rupert Horrox, courtesy of the Imperial War Museum, London) *cover* (top-left),
17 (top); Wayland Picture Library 11 (right). Logo artwork by John Yates.

**All Wayland books encourage children to read and
help them improve their literacy.**

✓ The contents page, page numbers, headings and index
help locate specific pieces of information.

✓ The glossary reinforces alphabetic knowledge and
extends vocabulary.

✓ The further information section suggests other books
dealing with the same subject.

✓ Find out more about how this book is specifically
relevant to the National Literacy Strategy on page 31.

CONTENTS

WOMEN AT WAR

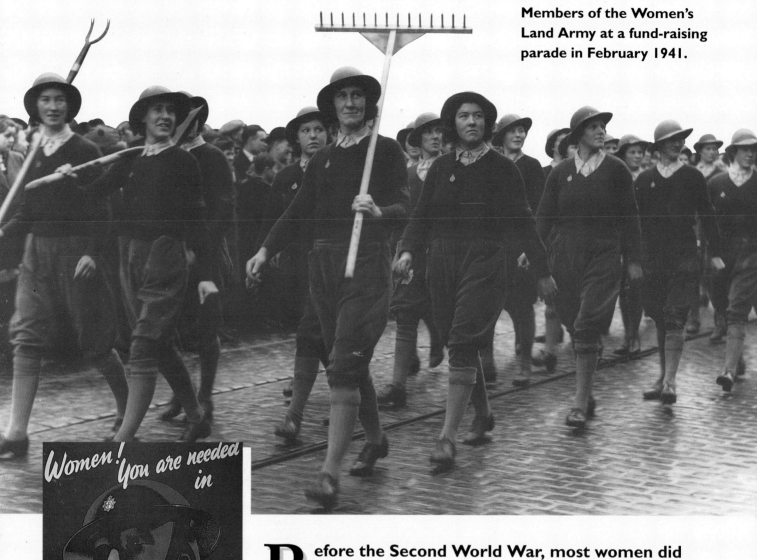

Members of the Women's Land Army at a fund-raising parade in February 1941.

A recruitment poster for the National Fire Service. Women did not fight fires, but worked as telephonists, despatch riders and cooks.

Before the Second World War, most women did not go out to work. Many people thought that a woman's proper role was to stay at home, looking after the children and doing the household chores. But when war broke out, men were conscripted into the armed forces. Women were now needed to do the jobs the men used to do. The lives of women would never be the same again.

For the first time, women were conscripted to help with the war effort. What kinds of job did they do? What was the Women's Land Army? How did women serve in the armed forces? There are many clues to tell us, if we only know where to look. By finding these clues, you can discover how women in your local area helped to win the war.

The history detective Shirley Bones will help you to find the clues you need. You should then be able to collect enough evidence and information to prepare and present your own project on women at war.

 The women in the photograph above are working in a factory in 1942. What do you think they are making? (You can find a big clue on page 28.)

Wherever you see one of Shirley's paw-prints, like this, you will find a mystery to solve. The answers can all be found on page 31.

A woman warden and medical officer join the search for survivors after an air raid.

DETECTIVE WORK

If you have female relatives who were adults at the time of the war, you could ask them about their experiences. This is called oral history, and it is an important way of gathering clues. Ask them if you can make a tape or even a video as they are talking. Try to find out how their lives changed during the war, and what kind of work they did.

FACTORY WORKERS

❖ Why do you think the workers in the procession described above wore coloured overalls?

Between 1939 and 1943, 1.5 million women took jobs in 'essential industries' such as engineering, chemicals, gas, water, electricity, shipbuilding, aircraft production and munitions. Some working-class women had already been working in factories before the war, but for women from the middle and upper classes factory work was a new experience.

Factory workers (right) in 1940, photographed taking their lunch break.

In March 1941, unmarried women between 20 and 30 were asked to register their current jobs with the local Employment Exchange. This meant they could be given suitable war work – which they had either done before, or could learn easily. The government could force women to take jobs or move to other ones. The files marked 'Council' at your local Record Office should contain letters from the government to local councils, telling them to conscript women for war work.

This worker is sharpening a saw in a steelworks in 1943.

Many women worked in munitions factories. The man in the photograph is probably the foreman.

DETECTIVE WORK

Visit your local reference library. Ask to use the microfilm viewer to look at wartime newspapers. You should be able to find advertisements trying to persuade women workers to take jobs in a particular industry. Shirley Bones has found one. Make copies of these adverts to use as illustrations in your project.

Women were paid less than men, and men in some industries felt that such cheap labour was a threat to their jobs. In many factories women workers faced practical problems, such as a lack of women's toilets. At the beginning of the war it was also very difficult for mothers to work in factories, because there were few nurseries to look after their children.

Women at work in a factory in 1944.

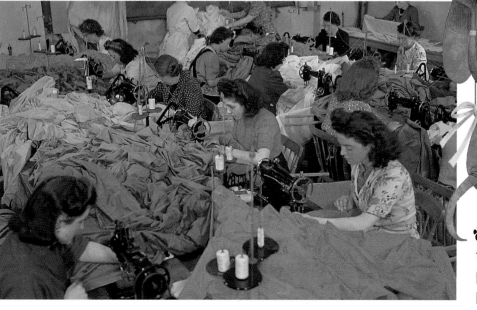

🐾 What do you think the women in the two photographs on this page are making?

HOUSEWIVES

Women who went out to work played a vital role in the war effort, but women who stayed at home did an important job too. Housewives whose husbands were away fighting looked after their families in very difficult circumstances. By taking care of their neighbours' children, housewives also made it possible for many mothers to take jobs in the factories and voluntary services.

Wartime shortages meant that everyday tasks became a real challenge. Food was rationed, and housewives had to spend hours queuing for their share. They then had to find ways to make the rations stretch, so that everyone had enough to eat. This involved growing their own food, and coming up with new recipes to use what food was available.

Housewives also helped the war effort by recycling. Scrap metal, waste paper, rags and leftovers from meals were all recycled to make up for the many shortages caused by the war.

A housewife collecting scraps in 1940, to be recycled as pig food.

✿ Look carefully at the photograph on the left. What sort of scraps did the council want for recycling?

PLACE YOUR
FOOD WASTE
HERE

EVERY
OUNCE
COUNTS

Clothing was rationed too. Women became expert at mending and altering garments, and also at making their own clothes. The government used adverts like the ones below to tell housewives how they could help the war effort. You may be able to find some by looking in old newspapers on microfilm at your local library.

An advertisement showing how needlework could help Britain to win the war.

✿ What can be used to make a pair of slippers according to one of the headings in the advertisement above?

DETECTIVE WORK
Try to find clues such as ration books, wartime recipe books or books giving tips on how to 'make do and mend', by rummaging around in junk shops and at jumble sales and car-boot sales. These books can give you an idea of what everyday life was like for housewives during the war.

Although they worked very hard, some housewives worried that they were not doing enough. They felt guilty about staying at home. The government disagreed. In 1940, it even released a film, called *They Also Serve*, which showed how important the role of the housewife was to the war effort.

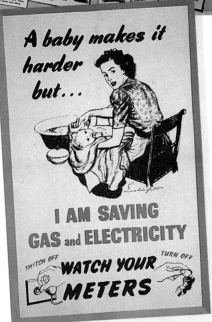

This advert asked people to save energy.

HOSTS

A host, Mrs Bryant, gives out clothes to evacuees living with her.

In 1939 and 1940, thousands of children were evacuated from areas that were likely to be bombed during German air raids. They travelled to places that the government thought would be safer. Women living in the safer areas did a very important job by offering homes to the evacuees. These women were known as hosts.

She's in the Ranks too !

CARING FOR EVACUEES IS A NATIONAL SERVICE

Evacuees' parents were supposed to pay for things like shoes and clothes. Some clothes were also donated by organizations such as the Women's Voluntary Service. However, many hosts used their own money to make life more comfortable for the children staying with them.

The poster on the left was issued by the Ministry of Health to show the importance of hosts.

✤ Who are hosts compared to in this poster?

The host in the photograph below, called Anne Norris, was awarded the British Empire Medal for looking after evacuees from London.

In Dorset, a Mrs Price took in seventeen evacuees. Although she received a lot of money for looking after the evacuees, her expenses must have been very high. Just think how long she must have spent in queues buying food for them all.

This poster called for more women to help with evacuees.

It was not only children who needed places to stay during the war. There were also many men and women in the armed forces living far from home, who needed billets. The newspaper cutting below is a vital clue telling us how much hosts were paid for giving board and lodging to soldiers of different ranks.

DORSET COUNTY CHRONICLE AND SWANAGE TIMES
7 September 1939

Soldier: Food and lodging 10d per night for one soldier, then 8d per night for others.

Officers, who would provide their own food: 3s per night for the first officer and then 2s a night for the others.

☙ If one ordinary soldier stayed at a house for 7 days, how much payment would the host receive? Remember, there were 12 pence (d) in every shilling (s).

DETECTIVE WORK
Place a notice in your community newspaper or village magazine, asking women who looked after evacuees or other people during the war to write to you. Their letters about their experiences would be excellent documents to have in your project.

Dear Shirley I have so many interesting things to tell you.....

TEACHERS

With so many men away fighting, there was a serious shortage of teachers. Women who had retired, or had given up teaching when they got married, were brought back to the classroom. Unfortunately, there was also a shortage of classrooms.

Evacuees from Rochester at a school in Sussex in 1941, having an outdoor lesson.

> At Leiston school, for one session each day, we had the use of one small room which we and our evacuees had to share with a Dagenham headmistress. We had no apparatus, no guidance as to what to do or teach ... We gradually acquired a small collection of reading books, paper, pencils and crayons ... The rest of the school day we had to play in the park or walk the children around the lanes and go to the woods.
>
> Win Elliott and Sylvia Lewis, in *I'll Take That One*

Many teachers were evacuated with their schools. Like the children, they had to leave their homes and families behind and learn to live with strangers. They often had to teach in classrooms which were shared with other schools, or even outdoors.

Even an Oxo tin could start an invasion scare.

One teacher created an invasion scare when she organized a treasure hunt for her class. The children were given strict instructions to destroy all the clues once they had read them, but one was found by a villager. It simply said 'Go forward 500 yards to a gatepost near the cottage. Look for Oxo tin and follow instructions inside.' The local people thought it was the work of spies.

✿ What do you think the pupils in the photograph on the right are doing, and why? Shirley has found a clue.

Teachers acted as parents to many evacuees. They made sure that the children were being well looked after by their hosts, and checked whether they needed new shoes or clothes. Some gave up their Christmas and other holidays to stay in school, so that children who were feeling homesick could come and talk to them.

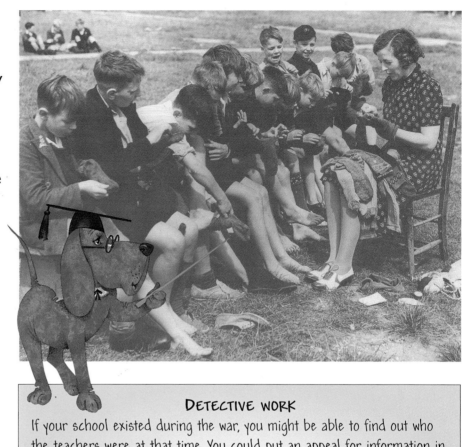

A teacher in 1940, taking a group of evacuees for a walk.

DETECTIVE WORK

If your school existed during the war, you might be able to find out who the teachers were at that time. You could put an appeal for information in the school newsletter or the local paper. Someone may even know where the teachers are living today, and you might be able to track them down. This is real detective work, and it is worth the trouble.

AIR-RAID WARDENS

Doreen Ellis, in 1999.

Every evening, air-raid wardens patrolled the streets making sure that no lights were showing during the blackout. If there was a bombing raid, the wardens guided people to shelters, set up first-aid posts and helped to rescue the injured.

Doreen Ellis was an air-raid warden in Maida Vale in north-west London. The following extracts are taken from an interview with her. She talks about her work during a heavy bombing raid on the night of 10 May 1942.

INTERVIEW WITH DOREEN ELLIS

The first thing we had to do after registering was to go out with a companion on 'lights' patrol, that was to check whether any light was showing on a certain patch. This particular evening a first-floor flat was showing a hall light. After finding out that there was no one in we found a ladder and climbed up to the first-floor balcony. We had to break in to turn off the light and then we left a note.

❉ Why was it important to make sure no lights were showing during an air raid?

INTERVIEW WITH DOREEN ELLIS

It was a very noisy night and we had several incidents and people coming in for shelter and first aid. About 1 am a doctor called in to help. I had difficulty in bandaging a knee and calf. I also put a tourniquet on a girl's wrist while out on patrol. She had passed out and I left her propped up sitting against a wall for an ambulance to pick up. She had a note on her good wrist saying who she was.

Doreen's story provides us with a lot of useful information about the work that wardens did. It helps us to imagine the effect the wardens' work had on their lives.

Rescuing a baby after an air raid in 1942.

Doreen's recollections of 10 May are very clear. She had recorded the events in her own diary, which is also a valuable source of clues.

Diary of Doreen Ellis

During this time several bombs had dropped. One sheered off a whole front of a block of flats and we had a steady stream of people coming in for shelter and first aid. A friend of mine was caught in the blast from a nearby bomb and was taken to hospital with many shrapnel wounds. The 'all-clear' went about 6 am and we were able to go home to bed, very weary. I got up at 8 am and went to work.

✿ What is shrapnel? You can find the answer somewhere in this book.

Imagine how exhausting it must have been to work through the night and then get up to do your normal job the next day.

DETECTIVE WORK

To create an interesting illustration for your project, take Doreen's account and make it into a strip cartoon. If you can find your own subject to interview, and then make it into a strip cartoon, that would be even better.

An air-raid warden and a nurse search for people trapped beneath rubble after an air raid.

VOLUNTEERS

Many women helped the war effort by doing voluntary work. The Women's Voluntary Service (WVS) was founded in 1938. By 1945, the WVS had over one million members.

A WVS recruitment poster.

Housewives!
W·V·S
needs your help!
Even if tied to your home you ca[n]
help the wardens and your neighbou[r]

A WVS mobile canteen. These canteens delivered refreshments to rescuers and survivors in areas damaged by bombing.

Voluntary workers were out on the streets every night during the Blitz, providing help and refreshments. Women working for the WVS set up mobile canteens to provide tea and sandwiches for exhausted rescue workers, victims of air raids, and people coming out of the shelters.

✿ Why do you think it was so important for the WVS to use mobile canteens, rather than setting up canteens in buildings?

4 am … We open the side of the van, let down the counter, get the mugs from the drawers, by the light of a very small electric lamp. Then out of the darkness appear pale faces, the faces of men, women and children looking up at us. The sound of distant gunfire is drowned by coughing and a clamour of voices: 'Tea miss … three teas, mate, and three nice cakes …' From our van alone my colleague and I serve in under three hours about four hundred cups of tea.'

Lorna Lewis, a worker in a mobile canteen, November 1940

Voluntary groups also helped combat war shortages. WVS members collected unwanted pots and pans, which could be melted down and recycled to make weapons and aircraft. They collected unwanted clothes, toys and household items to give to evacuees or to people who had lost everything in air raids. WVS knitting groups also made clothes and blankets to help keep these people warm in emergencies.

This badge was worn by the leader of a WVS group.

In the countryside, members of the Women's Institute (WI) were famous for making jam. They used fruit they had collected, and a special ration of sugar from the Ministry of Food. In 1940, five WI members in Kent with a canning machine produced 35 tonnes of canned fruit and 35 tonnes of jam.

A WVS knitting group in 1939. They met to knit clothes, and to make blankets out of squares of material. You can see one of these blankets on the table.

DETECTIVE WORK

If there is a WVS group in your area, write and ask where the minutes of wartime meetings are now kept. If you can get hold of these, you will be able to find out what your local group did during the war.

TRANSPORT WORKERS

After the introduction of conscription, there were not enough men to work in the vital areas of transport and communication. Before the war, few women had worked in these areas. Now they had to be quickly trained, in order to keep the country moving and to keep telephone switchboards working.

Many women were employed to operate the telephone switchboards at the centre of Britain's communications network. Others took on more unusual jobs as transport workers. Their tasks included driving tankers, and working as mechanics, railway guards and bus conductors. This was another example of women becoming accepted in jobs which before the war had been considered suitable only for men.

Mechanics (right) working on a petrol tanker in 1941.

This woman is acting as a signaller on a Yorkshire railway in 1941. She received only two weeks' training before she started her job.

I was troubled with uncertainty. Was it I who was going to dress up in conductor's uniform, run down to the tram depot in the blackout, shout 'Fares Please' [and] punch tickets ... Was this woman in navy blue myself?

Zelma Katin,
Clippie, The Autobiography of a Wartime Conductress, 1944

Women were fitted out with new uniforms, and quickly trained to work on the buses and trams. At first, women conductors seemed unusual, both to the passengers and to the conductresses themselves. Soon, though, nobody gave it a second thought.

Women bus conductors (right) working for London Transport in 1940.

A poster (below) advertising for bus and tram conductors.

Enjoy your War Work

GOOD PAY · FREE UNIFORM AND AN INTERESTING JOB

LONDON NEEDS MORE WOMEN BUS AND TRAM CONDUCTORS

SEE LARGE POSTERS FOR PARTICULARS

By opening up new areas of employment and challenging the idea that women could not do certain jobs, the war changed life for women in Britain for ever.

DETECTIVE WORK

There are many transport museums around the country. Your local Tourist Information Centre should be able to help you find out if there are any near you. You could write to the museum, or visit, and try to find out what different transport jobs women took on in your area during the war.

LAND GIRLS

The Women's Land Army (WLA) was set up on 1 July 1939, and by 1943 there were 87,000 members. These women were known as 'land girls'. They successfully performed hard, physical work on the land, and provided Britain with vital supplies.

Land girls worked on farms, and in forests, nurseries and market gardens. They were usually given four or five weeks of basic training, although some were given no training at all. Some land girls worked with dairy cows. To learn how to milk them, they used bags full of water, hung from a frame. This training was vital, as the extract below explains.

> A power cut meant that the whole dairy came to a standstill and the milking machines could not be used. All the men were called in to help with the hand-milking of forty cows. Here was where my milking training came in useful, the head cowman and myself being the only two people who had mastered the technique.
>
> Dorothy Charlton in *Land Army Days: Cinderellas of the Soil*

This machine for teaching land girls how to milk cows was called 'Clarissa'.

Looking after lambs was one of the more enjoyable tasks for these land girls in 1943.

Land girls worked very hard. Their tasks included ploughing, weeding, hoeing, muck-spreading, harvesting, digging ditches, trimming hedges, planting and digging up root vegetables, and looking after orchards. They worked long hours, and could take only one week's paid holiday a year. They were not given the same rights as women in the armed services, and the WLA became known as the 'Cinderella Service'.

✿ Why do you think the WLA was called the Cinderella Service?

My white, tender hands were a thing of the past. Instead they became rough and calloused ... I rolled into bed at the end of the day to lay like a stone statue, not daring to move in case the pounding [backache] transferred itself all around my aching body.

A. Ivy in *Land Army Days: Cinderellas of the Soil*

A recruitment poster (right) for the Women's Land Army.

❀ How is the image of a land girl shown in the poster different from the reality shown in the black-and-white photograph below and described in the document on the left?

Land girls, the Giles sisters, being instructed by the farmer who employed them in 1942.

'We could do with thousands more like you..'

JOIN THE
WOMEN'S LAND ARMY

DETECTIVE WORK

At your local reference library, use the microfilm reader to look in wartime newspapers for articles about the Land Army. You might also find advertisements for equipment and clothing for land girls.

SERVICE LIFE –
BEHIND THE SCENES

Separate branches of the army, navy and air force were set up for women to join. The Auxiliary Territorial Service (ATS) was the women's branch of the army. Women who wished to join the air force signed up with the Women's Auxiliary Air Force (WAAF). Those who preferred the navy applied to the Women's Royal Naval Service (WRNS), and were known as Wrens.

This recruitment poster was designed to show that a driver's job with the ATS could be glamorous.

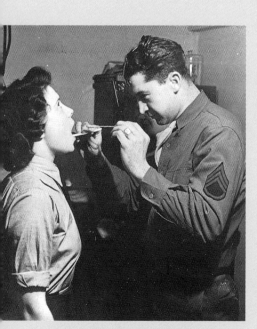

A WAAF officer is given a medical by an American officer in 1942. Many WAAFs worked with the US forces stationed in Britain.

ATS AT THE WHEEL

Ceaselessly new vehicles roll off the production lines.
Army units await them, the ATS deliver them

When the war began, most women in the services worked as cooks and clerks. Some worked in operations rooms as telephone operators and 'plotters'. Plotters in the WAAF moved markers on a large map to show the approach of enemy bombers.

Why do you think members of the Women's Royal Naval Service were known as Wrens?

The plotter moves her billiard cue again, and the counter approaches closer to our coast ... a WAAF telephone operator moves a switchboard plug, a message goes back to Command, and a few minutes later the siren wails in some coastal town. For that was the birth of an air-raid warning, in an operations room many miles from the raided town, and it was a WAAF officer who gave the word that set the sirens going.

Elspeth Huxley, WAAFS in the Operation Room, July 1942, quoted in Hearts Undefeated

You can see the plotter at work on her ladder in this photograph of a wartime operations room.

How do we know that this photograph was taken in, or after, 1940? (The clue is in the text on this page.)

Wrens also worked as plotters, to show the movement of naval ships and merchant convoys. At one command centre, in Liverpool, the map was on the wall and the plotters had to climb tall ladders to move the markers. In 1940, a Wren fell off and was killed. After that date, plotters all had to wear parachute harnesses hanging from the ceiling. You can still visit the command centre where the Wren's ghost is supposed to haunt the room.

DETECTIVE WORK

Look up the Army, Navy or Royal Air Force in the telephone directory. Find the address of its information office. Write and ask for information about women who served in the forces in your local area in the Second World War.

SERVICE LIFE – WOMEN IN ACTION

The role of women in the armed forces caused many arguments. People felt that the actual fighting should be left to the men. However, as the war went on, more and more service women performed roles that were close to the action.

Despatch riders at a training centre in 1943.

Women in the ATS took on many jobs. Some became mechanics, drivers and motorcycle despatch riders. Others worked as welders, carpenters and electricians. Women on the anti-aircraft sites perhaps came closest to fighting. Some directed searchlights at enemy bombers. Others prepared the anti-aircraft guns – but they were not allowed to fire them.

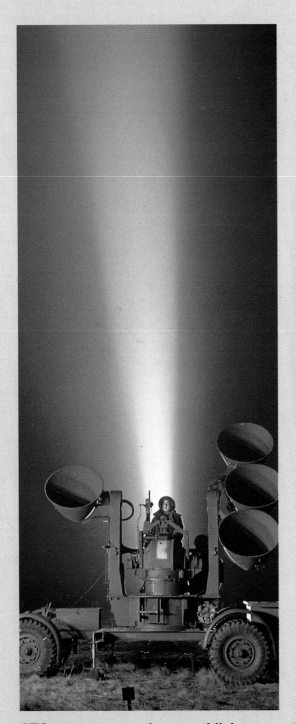

ATS women operating searchlights. Their job was to light up enemy bombers in the dark so that anti-aircraft guns could be fired at them.

Officers were instructed never to allow anything that would cause public outcry. Girls on the batteries were all volunteers, but if their parents objected they were posted elsewhere.

Leslie Whateley, director of the ATS

A recruitment poster for the WAAF.

Some women in the WAAF were trained as flight mechanics, but very few of them actually flew. Those that did transported Spitfires, Hurricanes and other aircraft from the factories where they were made, to the airfields where they were needed. Some women pilots transported large bomber planes. But the majority of women in the forces had to make the best of less exciting jobs.

🐾 What do the words of the poster on this page tell us about the different roles of men and women?

DETECTIVE WORK

Look through the local telephone directory, and try to find any local army, navy or air force museums. Telephone or visit the museums, and try to find out as much information as you can about women in the forces. See if there are any postcards for sale which could be used to illustrate your project.

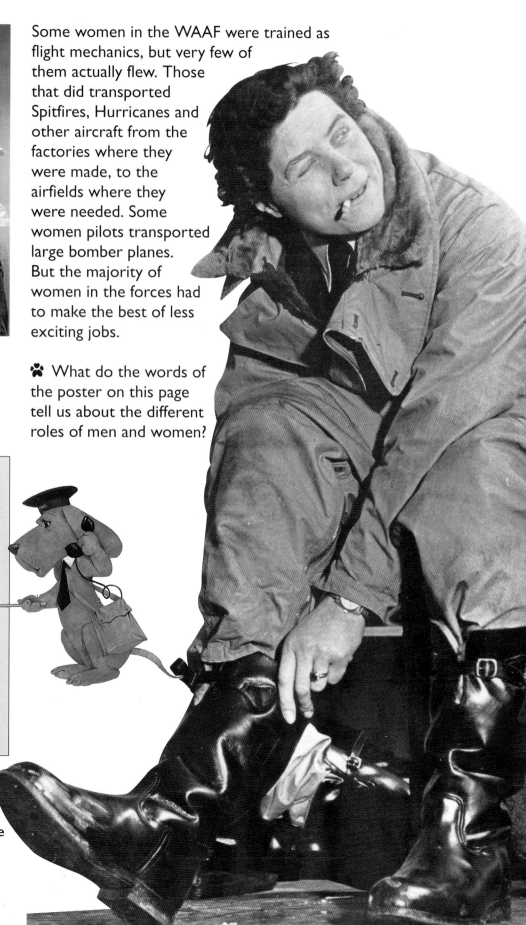

A pilot in 1940. Her job was to transport aircraft from the factories to the airfields.

NURSES

Extra nurses were needed to deal with the many wartime emergencies. Nurses had to work under very dangerous conditions. Some became service nurses, working abroad for the armed forces in military hospitals near battlefields. Others worked in British hospitals. They treated the injuries and illnesses caused by air raids, blackouts and wartime shortages.

Nurses at home and abroad worked in 'casualty clearing stations'. Here, the injured were given emergency treatment until they could be transferred to hospitals. The document below gives us an idea of the conditions nurses faced each day.

Nurses during gas mask training in 1939.

The men were lying in such a variety of positions, often with their limbs stuck out at queer angles in the plaster splints or sometimes slung on frames and hung with weights and pulleys; the light caught the glass flasks of blood which was still dripping slowly into the four bad cases.

Lena K. Chivers, a nurse at a casualty clearing station in August 1944, quoted in *Hearts Undefeated*

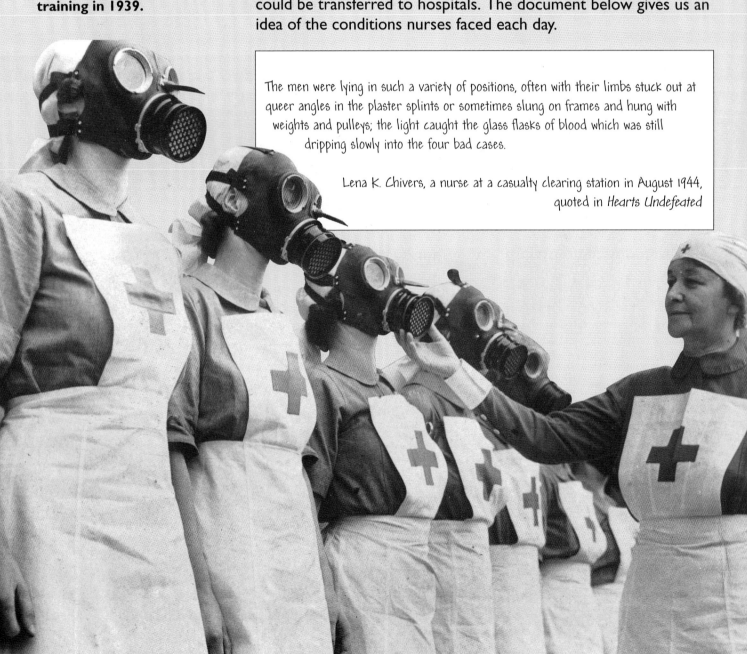

DETECTIVE WORK

Some large houses in the countryside were used as convalescence homes, where injured people were sent once they had started to get better. Visit your local Record Office and find out if there were any of these convalescence homes near you. Look up 'Convalescence Homes' under 'Wartime'. The archivist will help you.

Nurses on motorized bicycles called 'autocycles', in 1939.

During a bombing raid a hospital was just as likely to be hit as any other building. Some nurses found themselves working in operating theatres where the electricity kept going off and the ceiling was falling in around them. Between 1940 and 1942, 15 nurses were awarded George Medals for their bravery.

Of course, nurses still had to look after people with everyday illnesses. They also carried out health checks on evacuees. District nurses travelled from house to house, looking after people who were not sick enough to be in hospital. Many travelled by motorcycle or bicycle. They rode in the darkness of the blackout along roads littered with rubble from bombed buildings.

A George Medal, awarded for bravery.

Why would wartime nurses have travelled by motorcycle and not by car?

YOUR PROJECT

These service women in 1941 are tying down a barrage balloon. These balloons were floated high into the sky to prevent German bombers from flying low over their targets.

If you have been following the detective work at the end of each section, you should have found plenty of clues. These clues will help you to produce your own project about the lives of women in Britain during the Second World War.

Women were involved in many different aspects of the war, so you first need to choose a topic which interests you. You could use one of the questions below as a starting point.

Topic Questions
- How did women in the countryside help with the war effort?
- What was a day in the life of a land girl like?
- How did government posters portray women?
- How did voluntary workers help victims of air raids?
- What was it like to be a nurse in wartime?

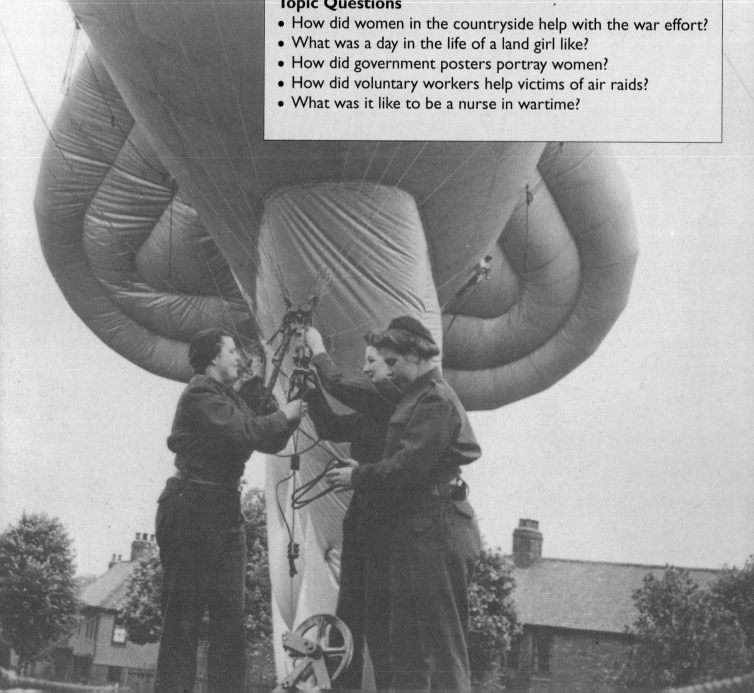

A government recruitment poster for women workers.

When you have gathered all your information, think of an interesting way to present it. You might like to use one of the ideas below.

Project Presentation
- Collect all the cuttings, advertisements and photographs you have found and produce your own newspaper.
- Write your project in the form of a diary.
- Produce a video or poster to encourage people to volunteer for war work.
- Divide your project into two halves, showing the contrast between women before and after the outbreak of war.

You might find an unusual subject for your topic. Shirley Bones found that some women helped to keep up morale during the war by entertaining people. There were female singers, musicians and comedians, who toured the country giving shows to troops and workers. Shirley even found a photograph of an ATS dance band.

An ATS dance band in 1944.

GLOSSARY

armed forces The army, navy and air force.

auxiliaries Workers who play a supporting role.

billets Accommodation, for soldiers or evacuees, in civilian houses.

blackout A period during the hours of darkness when no lights were allowed to be used.

Blitz The air raids launched by German bombers against Britain from 1940 to 1941.

calloused Hardened, for example where skin on the hands has been hardened by work.

civilian Not in the armed forces.

conductor/conductress Someone who collects fares and checks tickets on a bus or tram.

conscripted Forced to take part in wartime service.

contingents Particular groups, for example in an army or in a parade.

despatch riders Riders who carry important letters and messages.

evacuated Moved to an area of safety.

foreman A worker who supervises others.

merchant convoys Groups of ships carrying goods such as food and fuel.

minutes The official record of a meeting.

mobilized Prepared and put into action during a war or emergency.

munitions Military equipment, especially ammunition.

operations room A room where officers control military operations.

rationed Restricted, so that people can only have a certain amount each week.

shrapnel Small, sharp fragments scattered by a bomb, which can cause terrible injuries.

switchboard A system in a telephone exchange where calls are connected by hand.

tourniquet A tight bandage which stops the flow of blood.

tram A bus powered by electric cables which runs on rails through a city.

voluntary services Organizations run by volunteers, such as the WVS.

BOOKS TO READ

Hearts Undefeated edited by Jenny Hartley (Virago, 1994) This is a wonderful collection of women's writing from the Second World War.

I'll Take That One by Martin Parsons (Becket Karlson, 1999)

Quiet Heroines: Nurses of the Second World War by Brenda McBryde (Cakebreads, 1989)

Raiders Overhead: A Diary of the London Blitz by Barbara Nixon (Scolar/Gulliver 1980)

Wartime Women, edited by Dorothy Sheridan (Mandarin, 1991)

Children can use this book to improve their literacy skills in the following ways:

✓ To identify the many different types of text, and to understand the use of fact and opinion (Year 4, Term 1, Non-fiction reading comprehension).

✓ To use the Detective Work panels to prepare for factual research by reviewing what is known, what is needed and where to search (Year 4, Term 2, Non-fiction reading comprehension).

✓ To identify the features of a recounted text, comparing the air-raid warden's diary with her oral recollections (Year 5, Term 1, Non-fiction reading comprehension).

✓ To evaluate government advertisements for their impact, appeal and honesty (Year 4, Term 3, Non-fiction reading comprehension).

PUZZLE ANSWERS

Page 5:
☙ The women are making barrage balloons. These balloons were used to make enemy aircraft fly higher and so make it more difficult for them to bomb targets accurately.

Page 6:
☙ Coloured overalls gave the impression that their jobs and working conditions were attractive and exciting.

Page 7:
☙ The women in the top photograph are making hand grenades. Those in the bottom photograph are making parachutes.

Page 8:
☙ The council wanted scraps from vegetables, salads, meat, fish and bread, plus potato and apple peel. They did not want tea, coffee, the skins of grapefruit, oranges, lemons and bananas, or rhubarb tops. (Rhubarb tops make pigs very ill!)

Page 9:
☙ Slippers could be made out of an old felt hat.

Page 10:
☙ The advert compares hosts to people in the armed forces, showing that hosts have an equally important part to play in winning the war.

Page 11:
☙ The soldier would pay: 10d x 7 days = 70d. Divide this by 12 to convert into shillings and the answer is 5s 10d.

Page 13:
☙ The children are being shown how to darn their socks. Clothes were rationed, so it was important to learn how to mend old clothes.

Page 14:
☙ Lights could be seen from the air by bomber pilots, which made it easier for them to hit their targets.

Page 15:
☙ Shrapnel is the name given to metal pieces of bombs, which travel at high speed after a bomb explodes, killing and injuring many people. You can find this information in the glossary.

Page 16:
☙ Mobile canteens could deliver refreshments to the areas where they were most needed. Also, there was always the danger that canteens in buildings might be destroyed by bombing.

Page 20:
☙ It was called the Cinderella Service because the women often worked long hours in poor conditions without getting any thanks – just like the fairy-tale character.

Page 21:
☙ The poster makes the land girls' life look very clean, easy and comfortable. The photograph shows how dirty the job could be in bad weather – the land girls have clearly been working in mud. The document tells us how hard land girls worked.

Page 23:
☙ They were known as Wrens because the name of the women's navy was shortened to WRNS.
☙ We know the photograph was taken after 1940 because the plotter is wearing a parachute harness. As the main text tells us, plotters only wore harnesses after one of them fell to her death in 1940.

Page 25:
☙ The poster uses words which reveal that men will be in the action while women will play supporting roles. These words are 'Serve in the WAAF, with the men who fly'.

Page 27:
☙ Travelling by motorcycle or bicycle used less petrol – which was rationed because it was in short supply.

INDEX

Numbers in **bold** refer to pictures and captions.